# Executive Coaching for Managerial Excellence

*A roadmap for executives, human resources and coaches*

by

Michael Brenner

*AuthorHouse*™
*1663 Liberty Drive, Suite 200*
*Bloomington, IN 47403*
*www.authorhouse.com*
*Phone: 1-800-839-8640*

*© 2007 Michael Brenner. All rights reserved.*

*No part of this book may be reproduced, stored in a retrieval system, or transmitted by any means without the written permission of the author.*

*First published by AuthorHouse 7/10/2007*

*ISBN: 978-1-4343-0474-2 (sc)*

*Library of Congress Control Number: 2007902746*

*Printed in the United States of America*
*Bloomington, Indiana*

*This book is printed on acid-free paper.*

To Roberta, my best friend and wife of over thirty years, for all that I have learned from her that has enhanced my coaching skills

# Acknowledgements

This book has come about as the result of many cooperative efforts. First, Aspatore Publishing for whom I have published several commentaries raised the possibility which led me to proceed on my own. Next, my wife, Roberta, in addition to being encouraging, read both the first draft and the last draft and made helpful comments. The first editorial review was by my daughter, Samantha, in her winter break during her first year of an MBA program at Columbia University. She overhauled the organization of the material to make it a smoother read. Laura Larson Cage, who is a friend and an experienced book editor, also did a very professional review of this manuscript and made it PC, i.e. publishing correct. My son-in-law, Jon Kaufmann, who has a proofreading practice, was the final proofreader. Justin Axelrod from AuthorHouse was helpful in completing the publishing process. My colleagues from the New York Executive Coaching Network were helpful with encouragement and opportunities to clarify ideas.

This book is for:

1) Executives who want to consider coaching to break through barriers to success
2) HR executives who want to enhance management development
3) Executive coaches who want to enrich their practice

## *Comments about this book*

"This is a practical, intelligent book that offers sound guidance. It offers powerful tips and is well-grounded in theory. The case studies provide a down-to-earth road map for bringing managerial excellence to life."

Dr. Lynn Diamond, President,
Innovative Information Techniques, Inc.


"You have de-mystified executive coaching by showing it as a grounded and logical process with a bottom-line orientation."

Robert Krefting,
Management Consultant


"You clearly have significant working knowledge and experience in executive coaching."

Thomas Crane, President,
Crane Business Group, Inc.


"A great book"

Karen Staib Duffy, President,
Quantum Development Coaching

## *The Challenge*

For an organization to function, management provides the structure, direction and leadership to achieve the organization's mission. For organizations to thrive, managerial excellence is required. There are numerous best practices that are well-known to consultants, academicians and business executives. The *challenge* is to use the available knowledge of managerial excellence. Executive coaching is the best available tool to bring managerial effectiveness to life.

# Contents

### Chapter 1  Introduction
Introduction to Executive Coaching ...................... 1
The Four Cornerstones ........................................... 3
The Impact ............................................................. 6

### Chapter 2  Achieving Business Success
Barriers to Overcome .............................................. 9
Case Study: Developing Soft Skills ...................... 12
Introducing the Executive Coach ......................... 14
The Management Process ..................................... 15
Opportunities for Executive Coaching ................. 17
Managerial Effectiveness ....................................... 19

### Chapter 3  The Executive Coaching Process
The Process ........................................................... 25
Confidentiality ...................................................... 26
The Partnership between Coach and Executive .. 27
The Rules of Engagement .................................... 28
Roles and Responsibilities .................................... 31
Helping Changes Last .......................................... 33

### Chapter 4  Results
Measuring Impact ................................................ 37
Potential Pitfalls ................................................... 38
The Last Word ..................................................... 39

### Appendix A  The Coaching Process: A Step-by-Step Overview
Phase I (Months 1 – 2) ......................................... 41
Phase II (Months 3 – 6) ....................................... 42
Phase III (Months 7 – 9) ...................................... 43

## Appendix B  Case Studies
    The New Chief Executive Officers ...................... 45
    Battling with the Founder ................................. 45
    Leading a Start-up ............................................... 46
    The Technical Experts ........................................ 48
    Accepting Your Own Competence ..................... 48
    Transitioning from "Doing" to "Leading" ........... 49
    The Overwhelmed Executive .............................. 51
    The Team Leaders .............................................. 53
    Who Is Dysfunctional Anyway? .......................... 53
    Getting a Team to Click .................................... 54
    Getting an Executive on Board ......................... 55
    Getting the Successor Ready ............................. 56
    Enhancing Influence and Delegation .................. 58
    Improving Profitability by Changing Management Style ................................................................. 58

## Appendix C  Finding and Selecting a Coach

**Bibliography** ........................................................... 65

# Chapter 1
# Introduction

**Introduction to Executive Coaching**

Executive coaching is surrounded by a cloud of mystery which leads to reluctance among individuals and organizations to utilize this tool. This hesitation is in the face of significant acceptance of executive coaching as a means of enhancing individual and organizational performance. Its use has increased steadily over the past twenty years to the point that today, over half of the Fortune 500 companies utilize executive coaches.

Furthermore, The Conference Board, a bellwether of established business practices, has been running conferences on executive coaching since 2003. In addition, The Conference Board has a Council on Executive Coaching that includes organizations such as AstraZeneca, Capital One, Cardinal Health, Fidelity Investments, Ford Motor Company, Lockheed Martin, Marsh & McLennan, NASA, Unisys, United Technologies and Wachovia.

National media including the *New York Times* and the *Wall Street Journal* are periodically featuring articles about executive coaching. In the November 2004 *Harvard*

*Business Review* there was an article entitled "Wild West of Executive Coaching" by Stratford Sherman and Alyssa Freas of the Executive Coaching Network (www.excn.com). The article covers many of the challenges and risky elements associated with executive coaching. Also, the *Forbes* September 5, 2005 issue includes an article on "Quelling Your Inner Jerk" that describes CEO coaching by Marshall Goldsmith, the best-known and most established executive coach.

Still, the sense of mystery persists about this management development tool. For as long as organizations have been striving to do better, new management practices have been added to the available tools. From Henry Ford's assembly lines to the balanced scorecard, there has been no shortage of new ideas as to how to improve organizational effectiveness. Books and seminars abound; consultants tout these approaches to boost their clients' performance. Nevertheless, the knowledge of best practices and the introduction of new ideas have not stopped the search for the magic bullet, the way to really have an impact on the way businesses are run.

*So what is the missing link? Leaders, managers and people are the operational link between any idea and action. With all of the exposure to new approaches, something is missing. Basically, there is a gap between what we know and what we do. This gap is particularly notable in management practices.*[1] *Executive coaching is the best available tool to fill this gap.*

The core message of this book is that we have sufficient ideas regarding best practices for managerial

---

[1] J. Pfeffer and R. Sutton, *The Knowing-Doing Gap* (Cambridge, Mass., Harvard Business School Press, 2000)

(and hence, organizational) excellence. Nevertheless, leaders and managers struggle to apply these ideas effectively. Executive coaching is a personalized, tutorial system for individual managers. It can be viewed as the means to notably enhance their capacity to translate ideas and best practices into action and therefore organizational success.

Executive coaching is not therapy for managers. Even though 60% of the professionals providing executive coaching services have advanced degrees in psychology,[2] coaching and therapy have little in common. Therapy focuses on the past as a basis for understanding current behavior. In contrast, executive coaching is forward-looking to find new approaches to increase managerial effectiveness in the future.

**The Four Cornerstones**

Have you ever wondered why some organizations are successful and some are not? What does "success" mean, anyway? For a start-up, it means survival and getting a foothold in the business world. For a mature organization, the key issues are likely to be market share, profit margin and stock performance. The life cycle of organizations provides numerous examples of success side-by-side with stories of failure. Less than 10% of start-ups are still operating after two years. The few special successes like Microsoft and Google contrast with many thousands of start-ups that never grow past infancy. For the established companies, every industry grouping has industry leaders

---

[2] Benjamin Dattner, Dattner Consulting, New York, New York, Survey of Executive Coaching 2004.

and many also-rans. Why are some strong and others not?

The first premise of this book is that *people are the answer*. Every new product idea, every sales campaign, every financial restructuring, every operational achievement starts with one person's idea and initiative. Ideas are translated into action through a management process that includes planning, organizing, leading, and monitoring.[3] The success of organizations, then, is dependent upon people who provide the leadership and managerial effort that guide ideas to a productive implementation.

The second premise is that *businesses do not stumble or fail because of lack of good models or ideas, but rather because of flawed implementation of known best practices*. Elements of various management theories offer hope to increase effectiveness. Stephen Covey instructs executives to prioritize their activities so that the greatest attention is focused on those areas with the highest potential payoff.[4] Peter Senge advises executives to focus on harnessing the competence and knowledge of their subordinates.[5] Peter Drucker emphasizes the importance of clarifying roles and responsibilities.[6] These thought leaders, among others, give us countless ideas that, when implemented well, are powerful tools for increasing organizational effectiveness. Still, with all of these great ideas about leadership and managing readily available to executives, there has

---

[3] In many texts on management, monitoring is called "controlling."
[4] Stephen Covey, *The 7 Habits of Highly Effective People* (New York: Free Press, 1989).
[5] Peter Senge, *The Fifth Discipline: The Art and Practice of the Learning Organization* (New York: Doubleday, 1990).
[6] Peter Drucker, *The Practice of Management* (New York: Harper, 1954).

been no notable, aggregate improvement in managerial effectiveness. This shortfall is a result of the gap between knowing and doing.[7] It has been exacerbated by the painful overload of activities and challenging timetables that result in inadequate attention to the work of being a leader, which in turn leads to weak implementation of known best management practices.

The third premise of this book is that *most leadership development processes do not adequately prepare executives to lead and/or manage to achieve success.* The numerous books, training programs and educational offerings aimed at helping executives perform at a high level often present the best practices at a conceptual level, and do not put those concepts into motion on a day-to-day basis. Therefore, the methods learned in formal training settings have a modest impact relative to their potential.

The final premise is that *the learning process associated with leadership and management is unique for each individual, and at the executive level the most effective approach to professional development is a customized one.* This is where the executive coach comes in. Each executive brings a unique package of past experience (including formal or informal professional development to date), natural ability and professional aspirations.[8] With this unique fingerprint of development to date, each executive has a different readiness to learn about leadership and management. Translating intellectual concepts into on-the-ground approaches is very difficult. *The executive coach helps executives build the bridge from theory to*

---

[7] See Pfeffer and Sutton, *The Knowing-Doing Gap.*
[8] Daniel Goleman, *Emotional Intelligence: Why It Can Matter More Than IQ* (New York: Bantam Books, 1995).

*practice,* thereby enabling each executive to truly operate by the best-practices principles in a way that fits his or her individual style. In other words, a coach helps executives realize their full potential as leaders and managers.

## The Impact

A controlled study measured the impact of executive coaching as a tool to increase the effectiveness of classroom-based managerial training.[9] In this case, a group of top- and mid-level managers participated in classroom-based managerial training course intended to help them increase their effectiveness. Then, half of the group also received individual coaching over a two-month period.

After the program was completed, researchers measured the productivity associated with each executive as a manager. The managers who received only the classroom training increased their managerial effectiveness by 22%. In contrast, the managers who received both classroom training and coaching increased their managerial effectiveness by 88%. Clearly, this study demonstrates the impact on productivity of adding coaching to the development process.

Executive coaching can reduce the number of mistakes due to ineffective management which causes faulty decision making, poor prioritization, inattention to clarifying roles and responsibilities, inadequate motivation of key individuals, nonoptimal use of limited resources, and a failure to grasp changes in the environment to mention just a few of the many potential business and

---

[9] Gerald Olivero, K. Denise Bane and Richard E. Kopelman; "Executive Coaching as a Transfer of Training Tool: Effects on Productivity in a Public Agency" *Public Personnel Management* (Winter 1997).

managerial problems. This book is intended to provide an understanding as to what executive coaching is as well as some of the specific ways in which it can improve organizational effectiveness.

# Chapter 2
# Achieving Business Success

**Barriers to Overcome**

Let's look at a few situations wherein coaching was introduced as a means for overcoming barriers to success. Case studies on these and other real-life coaching scenarios are available in Appendix B.

- A vice president at a financial services organization had a brilliant record of exceptional innovation, but his interpersonal style did not support the personal connections required to be promoted to senior vice president. He was given feedback and acknowledged the need for a change in style, but he was making very little progress. (See case study on page 12)

- A newly appointed CEO of a small advertising agency that was part of a global advertising holding company was challenged by the presence of the agency founder, whose egotistical demands and narcissism threatened to undermine the continuing success of the agency. The CEO had operated under the founder for several years and had learned how to serve as a buffer between the founder and the increasingly restless senior management team. He facilitated an inspiring environment that led to a surge in growth after a period of flat performance for the agency. The founder was an in-your-face person, with no boundaries of when and where unpleasant outbursts were allowed. Furthermore, the founder started a twisted vendetta against the newly appointed CEO. The holding company group executive was not sure how to navigate the turbulent waters at the agency to allow the recently renewed success to continue. The newly appointed CEO needed support to neutralize the impact of the founder. (See case study: Battling with the Founder)

- A four-year-old start-up was struggling with a leadership vacuum. The founder is an extraordinarily bright individual who spotted an opportunity for a business-to-business transformation in an industry. The board of the company appointed a chief operating officer (COO) to serve as the center point of business and managerial leadership within the company, allowing the founder to pursue his vision and to continue relating closely to customers and investors. After one year, the COO was not filling the management vacuum.

*Achieving Business Success* 11

With the decision made to terminate the COO, what should the company do next? (See case study: Leading a Start-up)

- During the recent boom period in the mortgage business stimulated by the very low interest rates, one organization grew by a factor of 10 in each of two successive years. Individuals who were used to managing small teams of four or five people were suddenly given responsibility for 30 to 50 people spread out in multiple locations. The top underwriter was behaving badly in discussions with the CEO and in senior management meetings. Her performance as the head underwriter was outstanding in avoiding overly risky loans while approving the right ones. The loss rate from defaults was below the industry average and the company was growing rapidly. With no internal candidate to replace the head underwriter and the chore of recruiting a new head underwriter considered onerous, the company was not sure where to turn. (See case study: Accepting Your Own Competence)

## Case Study: Developing Soft Skills

This executive, a vice president with a staff of over one hundred people, was responsible for developing new approaches to very complex requirements using new technologies for a major financial institution. He clearly had an extraordinary ability for technological innovation. Furthermore, he was passionate about his work which led him to be intense and to dominate his staff. However, his most recent performance review noted his need to enhance his "soft skills" in handling people. His style was described as too fast-paced for some of his staff, who sometimes viewed him as too demanding. His contributions to the organization were commensurate with being promoted to senior vice president, but his interpersonal style was a barrier.

In addition to goals to become a better listener and to allow more time to build relationships with peers, one goal focused on increased use of influence to get ideas accepted rather than using a forceful approach. During this coaching engagement, he was encouraged to experiment with new approaches in dealing with people. For example, he was encouraged to try to be the "last voice" rather than the "first voice" when discussing complex technical issues. This change required enhanced listening skills and allowed his staff to develop ideas before hearing what the boss said. To build relationships with peers, he was challenged to have lunch once a week with someone at his level.

A notable insight came from a reorganization that was taking place during the coaching engagement. The number of his direct reports was being reduced from four to three and most of the responsibilities of the fourth direct report needed to be reallocated to the remaining three subordinates. The executive's normal style would have been to work on this reorganization independently of his subordinates and announce the new alignment of responsibilities. With the coach's encouragement, the executive asked his remaining three direct subordinates to help him solve the problem. When the final structure was agreed to and accepted, several decisions emerged that the executive would have not recommended himself because he felt that they were too controversial. However, the subordinates, with an open forum to discuss the new structure, wrestled with these issues and recommended the adoption of several potentially controversial restructurings.

The executive felt that he would have come up with a plan that was at least 80% identical to the ultimate plan that was developed with his subordinates' participation. He was aware that the solution was better than he could have accomplished on his own. The highest impact of this process was complete acceptance by his subordinates of the new structure. This learning experience of using influence rather than a forceful approach has become part of the executive's style by notably increasing the participation of subordinates in solving complex organizational issues.

As a matter of timing, just as the coaching engagement was drawing to a close, the executive was promoted to senior vice president. The promotion was a result of his modified interpersonal style that allowed him the reward of recognition for his substantial value to the organization.

- The senior vice president, technology at a growing Internet-based consumer service company was having trouble keeping her head above water. The 24/7 environment plus the demands from aggressive competition were making for endless days and a feeling of being overwhelmed. To add to her discomfort, several key elements of the company environment were getting on her nerves. What to do next? (See case study: The Overwhelmed Executive)

**Introducing the Executive Coach**

Enter the executive coach. Today's demanding business environment affords executives limited opportunities to devote time and energy to their own development as leaders. Most executives struggle to fulfill the responsibilities of their positions, and are too busy and too stressed to step back and learn from their experiences or to implement any changes to satisfy best management practices.

Cost pressures have led to flatter organizations wherein each executive manages a greater number of people than has historically been the case. "Speed to market" as a source of competitive advantage has engendered tremendous time pressure. Globalization has led to the use of many off-shore resources, which has created a whole new managerial environment. An increase in the number of working professional couples has reduced the support system at home, adding yet another overload. As a result, many of the basic principles of managerial effectiveness that are well-known and available are not applied by busy executives – even very capable, successful executives.

The day-to-day demands of the workplace limit the ability of talented executives to clarify priorities, delegate effectively, motivate subordinates and solve problems optimally. A major side effect of this harried environment is a loss of support for executive development. Few executives devote the time and energy to mentor others, and the informal feedback loop between manager and subordinate tends to be significantly underutilized. Without mentors to provide guidance, free time for contemplation, and effective management development mechanisms, executives are not improving managerial performance.

Executive coaching fills this void in today's frenetic business environment by elevating executive excellence as a strategic priority. Executive coaching is most useful for talented executives who may be falling short of their potential. The introduction of an executive coach can clarify the issues that need attention and guide an executive to a higher level of managerial excellence, leading to higher performance not only for the executive but also for the resources that he or she manages.

**The Management Process**

The primary aim of executive coaching is to strengthen an executive's effectiveness as a leader and manager. Generally, an effective executive experiences high job satisfaction. Also, an effective executive will have a well motivated team and less turnover. By extension, it can have a ripple effect throughout an organization.

Let's start by looking at the end-to-end management process to see where executive coaching can have an impact. Most MBA-level textbooks [10] describe some variation

---

[10] See, e.g., Stephen Robbins and Mary Coulter, *Management*, 7th ed. (Upper Saddle River, New Jersey: Prentice Hall, 2002).

on the following four building blocks of management. These distinct, but connected, activities are: planning, organizing, leading and monitoring. These four activities constantly interact as an organization operates.

**Planning** begins with the development of a vision and mission that serves as a guiding beacon for the organization as a whole. Using historical data and forecasts, a business plan lays out action steps to achieve the organization's stated goals. These goals serve as the basis to establish performance expectations in key areas such as sales, expenses, profit, quality, and service levels. All of the elements of planning are based on the best information available and provide guidelines of intentions. The best plans are not fat volumes that sit on bookshelves but concise, living, action-oriented documents that are updated regularly.

**Organizing** includes the allocation of roles, activities, and resources to clarify responsibilities across executives performing allied activities. Ambiguity about responsibilities is a common pitfall that can undermine executive effectiveness. Lack of organizational clarity leads either to overlapping efforts that are duplicative or to unfulfilled activities that "fall between the cracks."

**Leading** is the mechanism by which executives implement the plan to achieve the organization's goals. The core of leadership is making optimal use of human resources. Every person with management responsibility is ultimately responsible for the performance of his or her immediate subordinates and their teams. Leadership has many facets, and the best way of enhancing an executive's leadership effectiveness is unique both to the executive and his or her organizational circumstances.

**Monitoring** is the process of measuring performance relative to the organization's goals as laid out in the plan. An oft-cited maxim is "You cannot manage any activity unless you can measure it." That said, planning is an iterative process, and the monitoring process may open the door for midcourse changes to planned activities in light of emerging realities. For example, a failure to reach a profit goal may be corrected by restructuring responsibilities or assets (reorganizing), revising a plan to be more realistic, or taking a new approach to motivating a team to perform at a higher level.

## Opportunities for Executive Coaching

Executive coaching is, at the most basic level, a development tool for competent and talented executives. A survey by Right Management reports that over 86% of companies that use coaching said they do so in order to sharpen the skills of future organizational leaders as opposed to trying to correct underperformance. Whether it is a senior manager who is performing well but could do better, a high potential executive who needs broadening, a talented executive who lacks organizational savvy or an executive in a new situation who feels challenged by the scope of his or her responsibility, executive coaching is a valuable investment in the individual and for the organization.

On the other hand, executive coaching is not intended to turn around chronic underperformers. In general, executive coaching is not recommended for any executive whose continued employment at the organization is in doubt.

Specific examples of individuals for whom executive coaching can be high-impact include, but are by no means limited to, the following:

*Overloaded and overworked*
- An overloaded executive who is struggling to fulfill his or her responsibilities
- An executive who hesitates to delegate activities because they believe that they can do it faster themselves
- An executive who can not set priorities effectively and responds to the pressures of the moment without a focus on the highest-value activities

*Underdeveloped*
- An executive who is considered an appropriate successor to the next level in the organization, but who has a visible shortcoming in a key area such as management style, communications, interpersonal skills, or working with peers
- A high-potential, fast-track executive who has gotten a recent promotion that is something of a stretch
- Any executive from a technical discipline who has been promoted into a position that requires general management skills

*Authority challenged*
- A newly-appointed CEO who is not familiar with the authority, power and influence of his or her office
- Any newly appointed executive who is not comfortable with – or fully in command of – the responsibilities that go with his or her position

- An executive who struggles between making decisions independently and seeking ideas from subordinates for fear of losing control over the decision

*Relationship challenged*
- An executive who needs to enhance his or her effectiveness in dealing with peers
- An executive who has neglected the motivational impact of taking an active interest in subordinates' career development

*Organization building*
- A restless, high-potential executive who is a retention risk
- A newly-hired senior executive who needs to get up to speed quickly
- Any management person who needs to build a new team
- A long-tenured senior executive with strong past performance who has been in his or her position for an extended period and whose development has stagnated

The possibilities are endless and a complete list would encompass all of the developmental comments on all of the performance reviews that have ever been written.

## Managerial Effectiveness

*The power of the coach is not in creating new principles of effective management, but rather in applying well-known and well accepted managerial concepts to guide the executive to use these tools.*

Executive coaching can zero in on those elements of effective management that talented managers know they should do, but struggle to carry out due to time pressures and the like. An executive coach can bring these accepted principles to life in a manner that will dramatically boost organizational performance. Appendix B provides eleven examples of cases in which coaching enabled executives to overcome some of the challenging situations described earlier. Below are some basic tenets of managerial effectiveness on which a coach and executive can work:

*Clarifying mission* An executive may be managing a team that does not feel connected to the organization's mission even though it has been articulated. In organizations where such a disconnect exists, the coach can first identify the issue through the 360 survey and then work with the executive to develop action steps to ensure that there is full understanding of the mission.

*Defining priorities* Virtually every executive has more activities that are demanding his/her time than can be fulfilled. A coach might guide the executive through a simple, structured process of prioritization. For example, an executive may need encouragement to classify activities into A, B, and C categories with A including the important items that require immediate attention; B the important items that can be delayed; and C the other items that are not major and can wait. Almost always, defining priorities is the first step toward effective delegation as a way to reduce the demands on the executive's time.

*Clarifying roles and responsibilities* In today's environment, organizations are frequently restructuring businesses, departments, and jobs. Even a stable structure is subject to change through turnover. For a team to function at its highest level, there must be a complete and common understanding among all team members of each individual's role and responsibilities. Absence of clarity is an inhibitor to high-level team performance. A coach can identify this issue through the 360 survey. The coach can then keep it in the spotlight by setting a goal and facilitating action steps to clarify roles and responsibilities.

*Delegating* All executives need to delegate substantial activities and responsibilities. An executive is not the chief "doer" but rather the "facilitator of doing." To be effective at delegating, an executive needs to provide sufficient front-end guidance, set timelines for completion and communicate expectations regarding progress. As is the case for each of these elements of effective management, the how-to is well-known, but many executives have a difficult time in developing meaningful delegation practices. The role of a coach is to first encourage best practices; then help identify specific opportunities for delegation; and finally critique the outcome.

*Motivating subordinates* Groundbreaking and time-tested research has clarified the key factors in motivating employees. Herzberg[11], approximately fifty years ago, put a spotlight on recognition, achievement, responsibility, advancement, growth and work itself as the leading factors that result in satisfaction and motivation among employees. Conspicuously absent from this list is compensation, which has not been found to be a primary motivator.

The best way for any executive to leverage his or her impact on an organization is to maximize the productivity and effectiveness of immediate subordinates and their associated teams. The coach can guide the executive

---

[11] Frederick Herzberg, *The Motivation to Work*, (New York: Wiley, 1959).

through specific opportunities to use the principles of motivation, thereby enhancing the effectiveness of all their subordinates.

*Engaging subordinates in problem solving* The very core of an executive's role is problem solving and decision making. All executives are responsible for the impact of decisions that are made within their areas of responsibility. Many executives wrongly believe that enlisting subordinates in these processes is a sign of weakness and frequently fail to harness the competence embedded in their direct reports. Instead they rely too heavily on their own problem-solving skills.

The coach can encourage the executive to experiment with including subordinates in the process of solving problems on which the executive is deliberating. With direct reports involved in the process, the outcome is frequently improved, and the solution is readily accepted by subordinates, since they participated in finding it.

*Influencing peers and others in the organization* Frequently, an executive's success is highly dependent on his or her ability to influence peers or other people over whom they have no authority. Many talented executives do not know how to navigate this challenge. In the absence of authority, creativity is required in order to gain cooperation and collaboration. The ability to influence non-reports effectively can make or break an executive's success. This is a natural situation in which a coach can help an executive identify problem relationships, work with the executive to craft new approaches, and critique the effectiveness of early attempts to address problematic situations.

*Managing performance*   The weakest link in all managerial activity is performance management. Periodically, organizations develop new approaches to performance management with well-thought-out procedures and forms. Nevertheless, the human interaction involving assessment and feedback is handled in a woefully inadequate manner by the vast majority of executives. Here, the coach can guide an executive through several episodes of experimenting with new approaches to assessment of and feedback to subordinates. With this opportunity for the executive to practice and the coach to critique the effort, an executive can elevate the performance of his or her direct reports.

*Developing staff*   When considering the leading factors in motivating subordinates, it is apparent that every employee is very conscious of his or her own career development. This can take the form of simply wanting a promotion or feeling a hunger for more general development. Since employees always have this interest in mind, an executive can notably enhance the performance of any subordinate by acting as a mentor regarding each subordinate's career development. The coach can assist in creating a tailored approach to staff development for the executive and then critique the early efforts to add this element of staff motivation.

# Chapter 3
# The Executive Coaching Process

**The Process**

Executive coaching is not a quick fix. A typical engagement involves approximately forty hours of contact time (up to twenty five with the executive) over a nine month period. There are significant time requirements in the first two months for information gathering and goal setting, moderate time requirements in the next four months for action steps and trying new approaches and limited time requirements in the last three months for consolidation and reinforcement.

In the beginning, there should be a chemistry test to make sure the executive is comfortable with the coach. Then the coach gets oriented with background information from the executive, conducting a 360 survey of about 10 people, including his or her boss and frequently Human Resources. The executive, the coach, and the executive's manager work together to select up to three coaching goals. The bulk of the time is used to find action steps for the executive to take in order to achieve the goals. Progress is measured, and long term reminders are established.

It is recommended that, whenever possible, the early part of any coaching engagement be based on face-to-face meetings. However, once a relationship has been established between the coach and the executive, telephone calls becomes a very acceptable alternative to in-person meetings.

Appendix A is a detailed outline of a generic coaching engagement to provide a sense of the amount of time and resources required.

One of the most challenging questions surrounding the use of executive coaching is how to measure the impact of an engagement. Later on in this book, there are suggestions for measuring the payoff.

**Confidentiality**

In order for coaching to be effective, it is critical that the conversations between the executive and the coach are viewed as totally confidential. This means that at no time should the coach feel free to share with others any information that is gathered in the private conversations with the executive. However, at any point during the coaching engagement, the executive may give the coach permission to discuss any part of their conversations with relevant people. The only appropriate disclosure of confidential information is in the context of the early discussion among the coach, the executive, the executive's manager and a human resource representative about coaching goals. The goals are determined in part by feedback from two confidential sources – namely the 360 survey and a discussion with the executive. It is very important for the executive's manager to fully understand the coaching goals for the executive and to accept them or request changes.

The coach can report to either the manager of the executive or to HR two aspects of the coaching engagement. The first is the extent to which the executive is showing up for the appointments and cooperating with the schedule. The other item about which the coach can freely report is the extent to which the executive is engaged in the process.

The coach should be extremely careful in preparing the feedback report from the 360 to ensure that no person-specific attribution is possible. This element of confidentiality is particularly crucial, as failure to prepare the 360 report carefully can lead to disruption of important relationships for executives as they carry out their responsibilities.

## The Partnership between Coach and Executive

Successful coaching is built on a model of shared contributions and responsibilities for the coach and executive. This idea is presented well in the book *Co-Active Coaching*.[12] Putting this model in the business environment, it sees the coach bringing objectivity, forthrightness, focus, and commitment to the partnership. The objectivity comes from broad awareness of business structure and processes as well as familiarity with managerial behavior. Forthrightness is essential, and it requires the coach to be willing and able to confront an executive about any inappropriate action or behavior.

---

[12] Laura Whitworth, Karen-Kimsey-House, and Philip Sandahl, *Co-Active Coaching: New Skills for Coaching People toward Success in Work and Life* (Mountain View, Calif., Davies-Black, 1998)

The coach maintains the focus on the goals and action steps to reach the goals. This discipline keeps the partnership headed in the right direction. The coach's commitment to the executive's well-being must be total and uncompromising.

The coach also brings a wide range of business, organizational and managerial insights to the partnership. Therefore, during all discussions, the coach offers constructive suggestions based on past experience. This reservoir of knowledge is an asset to the executive but does not supplant the executive's responsibility to contribute to all phases of the coaching process.

For Co-Active Coaching, the executive is seen as creative, resourceful, and talented. The executive brings competence, self-interest, and, hopefully, humility. The competence encompasses functional business knowledge and experience. The executive has demonstrated his or her leadership and problem-solving abilities. Self-interest enables a balanced perspective regarding self-development and serving the organization. Humility entails total candor and critical self-examination to facilitate learning.

Together the coach and executive bring their respective resources to the table for the purpose of enhancing the executive's managerial effectiveness. The partnership requires building trust and mutual respect. Neither participant can be successful in this endeavor without the full engagement of the other.

**The Rules of Engagement**

Each executive coaching engagement is unique. The characteristics of the individual to be coached, the organizational structure and culture in which he or she operates, and the business challenges he or she face all define the specific situation. Still, some overarching principles are common to all successful coaching engagements:

1. **Commitment**. The executive must be fully engaged in the process and assume shared responsibility with the coach to achieve the goals set out early in the engagement. In turn, the coach must be deeply committed to maximizing the performance of the executive and the overall best interests of the company.

2. **Trust**. The working relationship between executive and coach hinges on complete confidentiality of all information that the executive shares with the coach. Therefore, the coach is only free to report on the extent to which the executive is engaged in the process, but nothing else without the permission of the executive.

3. **Partnership**. Successful coaching requires a full problem-solving partnership. The coach is responsible for being an objective and insightful facilitator. The executive must be candid, willing to try new approaches and eager to learn from positive and negative experiences.

4. **Goal-orientation**. The coaching goals are the engine that drives the engagement, and should be developed with input from all key stakeholders (including the immediate manager, HR, peers and subordinates). The maximum number

of meaningful goals for an executive coaching engagement is three. More than that is too ambitious and will dilute the effort to achieve sustainable change.

5. **Action learning**. Once coaching goals have been established, the coach and executive jointly develop an explicit action plan to achieve those goals. These actions serve as practice for new approaches. At each step in the engagement, the executive should review outcomes with the coach to assess his or her success in meeting the goals and identify any midcourse corrections.

6. **Candor**. The coach must be equipped and prepared to confront the executive in a constructive and professional way whenever the executive is operating in an inappropriate manner that undermines best performance.

7. **Measurement**. A measurement process should be established at the beginning of the coaching so that the executive and his or her immediate manager can determine whether the coaching goals have been accomplished.

8. **Sustainability**. All coaching should cultivate sustainable changes for the executive. Since the coaching ends at some point, the executive's changes should not be dependent on the coach's ongoing presence.

Attention to these principles will lead to a meaningful and productive coaching experience.

**Roles and Responsibilities**

In coaching as in business organizations, people are the key to success. For any coaching engagement there are three critical participants: the coach, the executive and the immediate manager of the executive. Let's look at success factors for each player.

The coach must have highly developed interpersonal skills. The coach will interact not only with the executive and the immediate manager of the executive, but also with other executives in conducting the 360 survey. The likely diversity of styles and personalities that the coach will encounter requires that the coach have a flexible style in order to interface successfully with this diverse roster of people. In dealing with the executive, the coach must be able to confront and/or challenge the executive in the process of finding new managerial approaches for the executive.

The coach must also have a broad understanding of organizations and people. Since management is all about organizations and people, the coach must be able to quickly understand the circumstances of the executive. The coach may have obtained these insights from working in organizations or from providing services such as consulting to organizations. Knowledge of the specific industry is not critical.

While coaching is to some extent an art, there is a structure to the process with which the coach must be familiar. Establishing the rules for the coaching engagement (confidentiality, partnership, goal setting, action planning) creates the framework for the entire coaching relationship. With all the frailties of measuring the effectiveness of coaching, the coach should provide leadership in finding an acceptable method for evaluating the effectiveness of each engagement (more on this later).

The executive is best served by approaching the coaching engagement with a positive mindset, viewing it as an opportunity for self-development. The executive gets the opportunity for confidential conversations with an executive coach and a safe place to explore sensitive issues. Sometimes, an executive sees the utilization of coaching as an implied criticism of his or her performance. Usually, the opposite is true. The organization sees the executive as a talented member of management and believes it is an appropriate investment to provide the developmental support of a coach for the executive.

The executive must be willing to share information openly. Other than the interaction with the manager of the executive and the 360 survey, the coach relies heavily on the executive for information. Therefore, the executive enhances his or her value from the coaching engagement by providing full disclosure of what is happening.

Since the coaching process is intended to stimulate change for the executive, he/she must be open to trying new approaches. Then, the executive must be willing to experiment with new approaches and report the results of each effort.

The executive's boss is a key figure in the success of any coaching engagement. The executive's boss sets the tone at the start of the engagement and can facilitate the attitude that coaching is an investment in a valued member of the team. The executive's boss is also a primary source of information and insights regarding the executive's strengths and areas for development. When the coaching engagement is completed, the executive's boss has the opportunity to continue to reinforce actions and behaviors that support the coaching goals.

Beyond the impact of these three people, the upfront process of selecting an executive to be coached may be the singularly most important step in determining success. Throughout this book are direct and implicit indications of criteria for selecting candidates for coaching. Executive coaching is more suited for talented and strong executives rather than average or weak performers. Success (which is not guaranteed) requires thoughtful selection of individuals for executive coaching.

**Helping Changes Last**

Extra steps are required to sustain positive changes from a coaching engagement. The purpose of the last three months of a coaching engagement is to reinforce the continued attention to the new approaches.

One approach that has proven valuable is to create a set of tailored guidelines near the end of the engagement. The guidelines encapsulate the meaningful lessons learned by the executive during the coaching and serve as a succinct reminder to the executive of new approaches that have been successfully implemented during the engagement. With ongoing discipline on the part of the executive after the engagement, these guidelines provide reinforcement to the positive changes that have come about during the coaching experience.

The guidelines should reflect the coaching goals. Typically, each executive will develop between five and ten guidelines. Examples of guidelines from real coaching engagements include the following:

- Enhance listening skills by always ensuring accuracy regarding what is meant by that person speaking to me. I should understand a question or get more depth as to the meaning of their statement before I respond.
- Reduce the usage of technical language and jargon when I speak to senior management and keep the focus on the impact of technology as opposed to the details of what technology does.
- When I do not understand something, don't guess, but ask questions for clarification.
- Use positive language rather than critical comments when trying to persuade someone without com-promising my commitment to influence them.
- Manage subordinates according to their actual competence rather than my standard as to what their competence should be.
- Recognize others and let them know that I appreciate their contribution(s).
- Don't be afraid to ask my subordinates for help in solving a problem.
- Believe that my development and continued learning will increase my value to the organization.
- Coach my direct reports regularly with discussions about their career aspirations, their developmental interests, their barriers to task achievement, their

personal life as it may be impacting them at work and their morale as a means of enhancing their effectiveness in fulfilling their responsibilities.
- Avoid confrontations when driving to get a task accomplished by asking numerous questions so that I understand the other party's needs. Make sure that the source of resistance of another person is understood and that reasonable accommodation is considered.
- Define, implement, and continuously adjust work/life balance that is appropriate for me.
- Continuously review my calendar (weekly) to ensure that I use my time for the high-value activities and to ensure maximum delegation of activities to direct reports.
- Concentrate on issues that I can control as a means of influencing issues that I cannot control.
- Interact with others in a humanistic manner as part of the process of solving problems.
- Don't be reluctant to toot my own horn or get recognition for my team.
- Celebrate my successes. Balance my self-critical tendency caused by high standards for my own performance with acknowledgment of the positive feedback I get from others.

- Develop effective working relationships with my peers as an important factor that will impact my ability to perform at a high level.
- Recognize that high performance in my job is enhanced by clarity about my career.

Each executive coaching engagement has its own pathway. The guidelines will be unique for each executive.

# Chapter 4
# Results

**Measuring Impact**

So what is the value of executive coaching? Let's look at some information about the payoff from coaching and approaches to measurement.

In 2001 a consulting firm by the name of Manchester conducted a survey on the perceived return on investment (ROI) for executive coaching.[13] This study surveyed over one hundred senior executives from mostly *Fortune* 1000 companies who had participated in executive coaching programs that were six months to one year in duration. Participating executives were asked to estimate the value of the coaching they had received. These estimates were then compared with the cost of the coaching programs.

Overall, the average perceived ROI was 570% – that is, the perceived value of the investment in coaching was

---

[13] Joy McGovern, Michael Lindemann, Monica Vergara, Stacey Murphy, Linda Barker and Rodney Warrenfeltz, "Maximizing the Impact of Executive Coaching: Behavioral Change, Organizational Outcomes and Return on Investment," *The Manchester Review*, Volume 6 Number 1, 2001

5.7 times the cost. The range of estimates of perceived value ranged from less than $100,000 to as much as $1 million. Over 90% of the executives who were coached indicated that the value received from the coaching was clearly greater than the time and money invested.

For the organizations in which several executives were coached, tangible business results were reported such as increased productivity (53%), better quality (48%), greater organizational strength (48%) and better customer service (39%). There were also reports of intangible results such as better relationships with subordinates (77%) and supervisors (71%), improved teamwork (67%), better relations with peers (63%) and greater job satisfaction (61%).

Measuring the impact of coaching is essential, but not simple. If return on investment cannot be meaningfully measured, other approaches are possible. One is to assess progress relative to the engagement-specific coaching goals, with the executive's boss as the chief arbiter of results. Another approach is to diplomatically return to the people who contributed to the 360 survey and ask for their observations of any changes. This measurement process should center on general observations about changes without focused inquiry about specific coaching goals, as identifying the coaching goals would be a breach of confidentiality.

**Potential Pitfalls**

What the executive gets out of coaching will be a reflection of what he or she puts into it. In addition to the success factors described earlier, it is important to be aware of a few key potential barriers to successful coaching.

*Maintain realistic expectations*  An unrealistic expectation about the capacity of any individual to change is one sure path to an unproductive executive coaching engagement. Just as a short person cannot be coached to be tall, a type A, intense and hyperactive person will not be transformed into a mellow, gentle executive. There is no checklist to define who should and who should not be a candidate for executive coaching. Certainly, an executive whose continued employment is in doubt is not a good coaching candidate. Nevertheless, the coach, the HR executive, and the executive's boss need to weigh this decision thoughtfully.

*Find the right coach*  Not all coaches are created equal, and chemistry is an important element of coach selection. While many organizations express a preference for somebody with knowledge of their industry, that is rarely an essential ingredient. However, an inexperienced coach may struggle. If the chemistry between the coach and the executive never gels, it may be a reflection on the coach. If the coach is too focused on being the expert and the superior in the relationship with the executive, the coach is inappropriate. See Appendix C for more on selecting a coach.

**The Last Word**

If people are the answer, then thoughtful and thorough attention to the activities of the important leaders and senior managers makes eminent sense. It is interesting that not only are people the answer, but a person, in the form of a coach, is part of the solution.

# Appendix A
# The Coaching Process: A Step-by-Step Overview

**Phase I (Months 1 – 2)**
- Conduct an initial one-hour meeting with the manager of the executive to be coached to describe the program, to get an initial view of key issues, and to set expectations.
- Hold an initial one-hour meeting between the coach and the executive to allow the executive to determine his or her comfort with the coach (the chemistry test), to explain the program and describe the confidentiality associated with coaching.
- For the coach, receive a detailed briefing given by both the manager of the executive and the relevant HR executive in order to specify the key measures of performance excellence for the executive and any notable barriers to achieving excellence.

- Have a two-hour meeting between the coach and executive to familiarize the coach with the executive's background and to begin to develop the specific goals.
- Conduct an interview-based 360 survey about the executive to identify key issues by speaking confidentially with approximately six to ten relevant people such as peers, subordinates and others with whom the executive does or will interact regularly.
- Deliver written feedback to the executive from the 360 survey with no direct attribution as to who said what. This feedback report is seen only by the coach who prepares it and the executive being coached. This information serves as a basis for further refinement of the coaching goals and development of the initial set of action steps to achieve the coaching goals.

## Phase II (Months 3 – 6)

- Complete the development of no more than three coaching goals. The coaching goals are then reviewed with four people together - namely the coach, the executive, the executive's manager, and a representative from Human Resources – to be sure of agreement as to direction and expectations.
- Refine action steps and implement the coaching plan. (This step involves multiple meetings over several months and represents the bulk of the time for the coach and the executive to work together.)
- About halfway through the engagement, get feedback from the executive's manager regarding visible progress and any additional considerations.

➢ Ask the executive to summarize lessons learned during the coaching to establish some guidelines as a reminder to the executive as to new practices, behaviors and styles that have been added to the executive's portfolio for leading and managing.

**Phase III (Months 7 – 9)**
➢ Monitor the executive's continued attention to the coaching goals and lessons learned.

# Appendix B
# Case Studies

These are summaries of real coaching engagements. In each case, some changes have been made to protect the identity of the individuals and the companies.

## The New Chief Executive Officers

### *Battling with the Founder*

At a small advertising agency that was part of a global advertising holding company, the agency's founder, who had built the business and sold it to the conglomerate, was behaving in a manner that was demotivating many of the senior executives. The conglomerate management decided to appoint a new CEO and chose the COO of the agency who had worked under the founder for several years. At the same time, the founder was kicked upstairs as non-executive chairman. The conglomerate was concerned that the former COO might be overwhelmed by the founder who was unhappy with the role as non-executive chairman. A coach was engaged to facilitate the transition of the COO into a full-functioning

CEO so that he could, in fact, run the agency with no interference from the founder.

This coaching engagement had a very singular focus. The goal of the coaching had been established by the conglomerate restructuring of the positions for the founder to non-executive chairman and former COO to CEO. In this case, the coach served two valuable roles. First, the executive – namely the newly appointed CEO – needed an opportunity to vent significant frustration regarding the behavior of the founder. Secondly, the new CEO needed to identify specific action steps that would achieve the goal of minimizing the effect from the founder while at the same time guiding the agency to growth in revenue and profits. Over several months the coaching maintained this singular focus. The coach continuously reviewed the executive's current activities involving the founder to help identify the appropriate action steps.

This reorganization of the top executives has resulted in a new burst in revenue growth and profits for the agency. This positive outcome reflects the effective managerial style of the newly appointed CEO and his effectiveness in isolating the impact of the founder. The coach's contribution was to reinforce the resolve of the newly appointed CEO to exercise the power and authority of his new position.

### *Leading a Start-up*

A start-up with about four years of experience, and approximately one year away from positive cash flow, was experiencing a significant leadership problem with the founder and CEO. The CEO was a Ph.D. and former college professor who had spotted an extraordinary business opportunity that he was developing successfully. The company had substantial financial backing from its industry and had grown to approximately twenty employees. While the CEO was excellent at pushing forward the new business idea as well as raising capital, he was uncomfortable with the position as top executive and had no built-in framework regarding basic managerial requirements such as clear definition of roles and responsibilities, effective delegation and performance management. To fill this gap, the board encouraged the company to appoint a COO which was done. After approximately one year during which the COO created bureaucracy and did not add to the managerial effectiveness of the organization, it was decided to terminate the COO and engage a coach for the CEO.

The coaching engagement included all the steps described in Appendix A for a typical coaching situation. The most critical element was the 360 survey. The written feedback report cited "the unanimous wish for you to accept the mantle as CEO which could show itself in the following ways: acting more quickly on difficult decisions regarding people; taking steps to eliminate conflict; putting energy into defining the organization structure; making a continuing effort to clarify the authority of each person." Working on these issues brought notable changes to leadership and management style for the CEO which resulted in his acting and feeling like a CEO. His new actions and approach to his role as CEO led to many favorable changes in the organization as a whole.

## The Technical Experts

### *Accepting Your Own Competence*

A very bright woman who lacked a college degree had worked her way up rapidly in the underwriting department of a mortgage company to become senior vice president, Underwriting. She was responsible for setting credit policy, directing the activities of approximately fifty underwriters and acting as the final reviewer of mortgages that fell outside the credit policy guidelines. She consistently exhibited excellent analytical skills, the appropriate toughness to turn down mortgages that had too many questions and a willingness to work very hard on behalf of the company. In spite of these positive qualities, she was prone to emotional outbursts that were unpredictable and disruptive to the work environment. In the early discussion with the coach, she described herself as a drama queen.

During the course of the coaching engagement, there was a detailed review of the excellent underwriting record for which she deserved credit. While it was easy to find external measurements that confirmed the high quality of her work, the president of the company (to whom she reported) spent very little time, if any, acknowledging the quality of her work. It became clear that a core human need was not being satisfied: acknowledgment for her good work. Since it was unlikely that any part of the coaching engagement would change the president's style and behavior, considerable effort was made during the coaching to establish self-monitoring mechanisms to continue reinforcing her ongoing awareness of the high-quality work she was producing.

This executive was also plagued by inadequate feelings because of her lack of a college degree, her young age and her responsibility for managing so many people. The coaching to counter these issues required building respect for the organization's judgment in appointing her to the senior position that she occupied. When she accepted the validity of the process that allowed her career to flourish her emotional outbursts substantially declined. As an epilogue to the coaching, it is nice to report yet another step in her career. When the mortgage company was acquired by a larger company, the acquiring firm was so impressed with her record in underwriting that she was not only retained but given expanded responsibility.

### *Transitioning from "Doing" to "Leading"*

This executive was newly promoted to director, Project Management, and had six direct reports, each a manager in Project Management and each with six project managers reporting to them. The director had been selected for this position because of her stellar ability to manage projects effectively. Many of her direct reports had been peers until her promotion.

The most important single issue for this executive was to stop being the individual who solved every problem and to become the executive who facilitated the solving of problems. At the start of the coaching engagement, her decision-making style involved gathering information, identifying alternative approaches, evaluating two or more possibilities and then implementing the approach that she felt was most desirable. This style led to her being a bottleneck in getting problems resolved. She was overloaded and her direct reports were frustrated because of her busy schedule. All this was compounded by the fact that there were several unfilled positions on her team. She was partially filling in to cover the responsibilities that were intended to be handled by people to be hired to the vacant positions.

For this executive it was very important to establish a sense of urgency around filling vacant positions. All of the tasks associated with this effort were examined and the coach encouraged the executive to find other resources to participate in the process. For example, instead of this executive personally screening all of the résumés that were being provided by Human Resources, batches of five or so were given to each direct report to evaluate. For each candidate that seemed attractive based on the résumé, a short list of important questions was developed and a Human Resources representative was asked to conduct a telephone screening of the lead candidates. The responsibility for initial screening interviews was again distributed among her direct reports. With these new approaches and a few others, the vacant positions were filled in short order. With a full complement of resources and a broader use of delegation, this executive was no longer overloaded and functioned as a more effective manager.

The area of personal and professional development for both the executive and her direct reports also became a topic of interest. Since personal growth and advancement are significant motivators, the executive was encouraged to schedule one-on-one time with each direct report to develop an understanding of their aspirations and to help each subordinate take steps to achieving his or her goals. Furthermore, the executive was introduced to the legitimacy of being proactive regarding her own development and growth. By recognizing the motivational aspect of development, this executive was able to understand the importance of growth and advancement for her subordinates.

**The Overwhelmed Executive**

For a company that provides Internet based services, this senior vice president Technology managed approximately one half of the one thousand employees at the company and self-initiated this coaching engagement. The issues that this executive highlighted in the early discussions included work/life balance, discomfort with some elements of the culture at the company and a general sense of being overloaded. The coach did not conduct a 360 survey but did have available the results of a recent, company administered, 360 survey about this executive. This coaching engagement centered on building a set of principles that could provide guidelines for this executive. A total of six principles were finally adopted that collectively addressed the issues that were identified at the start of the engagement.

The coach took the stance that as manager of half of the organization, the executive had to accept responsibility for the culture in her part of the organization. Then, to address the executive's discomfort with that culture, the following principle was adopted: I am in a position to define and change the work environment. The coach worked with the executive on identifying specific behaviors in the organization that caused discomfort to the executive. For example, there was excessive use of e-mail with the sender and receiver separated by only a few feet. Dealing with immediate subordinates, the issue was discussed, guidelines were developed, and specific expectations established. The result was more telephone and face-to-face interactions among team members. This change led to fewer misinterpretations and better relationships within the team.

One source of overload was a tendency to accept new work without fully recognizing whether it was appropriate for her and her organization to try to satisfy the request. Another was failing to recognize the amount of resources required to satisfy a request. The following principle was constructed to manage this challenge: Before responding to any request, I will get clarity as to what is needed and what is expected of me. By introducing this step, the executive was able to assess each request more fully and in some cases redirect the request to a more appropriate executive within the company.

On looking at work/life balance, the coach challenged the executive to select one evening a week when the executive would leave the office at approximately 5 p.m. At first the executive resisted, claiming that it was nearly impossible. Then, there was willingness to try this action once. Two important things happened to the executive. First, nothing bad occurred as a result of her not being there past 5 p.m. on that first try. Second, because of the clear intention to leave promptly at 5 p.m., the executive was better organized and more disciplined about the use of time throughout the day leading up to the early departure.

Three other principles were developed that in combination with those already described fully satisfied all of the initial concerns for this executive.

## The Team Leaders
### *Who Is Dysfunctional Anyway?*

At a small advertising agency that was part of a larger communications services corporation, this senior vice president, Account Services was having substantial friction with two of her direct reports. Attention from the agency CEO and intervention from HR were not working. The coach was engaged to improve this situation. After completing the 360 survey, it was clear that there was a very high level of dysfunction in the team being managed by this executive. The coaching engagement was enlarged to include some team coaching in order to address the team issues.

The team coaching effort had a clear spotlight on the difficulties. When two sessions were completed with modest progress, some unexpected events took place. One direct report was transferred to another team and then left the company shortly thereafter. A second subordinate also left the company. The meetings for the coach and executive had been totally focused on effective management of subordinates. Suddenly, the members of the team were different as new people were hired to replace the two who had departed. At this point the focus of the coaching shifted to building effective relationships with new subordinates, while being mindful of the information from the 360 feedback. This agency team was transformed from a dysfunctional one to a model team within the agency.

As a postscript, the two departed direct reports both left their new positions within months suggesting the possibility that the team dysfunction was more a reflection of these two people than the senior vice president.

Nevertheless, the coaching helped the executive through a difficult time and helped the agency retain a valued executive.

### *Getting a Team to Click*

This recently appointed regional sales manager was responsible for a sales team covering a well-defined region that included important clients of his firm. He had an excellent record as a salesman and as a key account representative. At the outset, it was clear that he was relentlessly focused on doing the best possible job for each client in order to enhance the company's sales results. The product required technical support and this regional manager was dependent on a parallel organization of engineers who were vital to successful installation of the company's products.

The primary problem that undermined the regional sales team's performance was the tension generated by the expectations of the regional sales manager. He was impatient with his sales representatives because they did not approach their work with the same gusto and commitment as he had demonstrated as a sales representative. This situation was further exacerbated because he showed the same impatience toward the engineering staff as he showed toward his own team.

This executive needed to learn how to be a manager and motivate high performance rather than be a negative and, at times, an angry micromanager who was critical about everything that was not being done well. He showed no awareness of a need to change his behavior in order to upgrade the performance of both the sales and engineering teams.

The coaching effort here led the executive to change his approach to managing his team. He accepted the responsibility for getting the team to perform well. He made a detailed examination of the sales staff to identify the level of competence for each person on the team. Developmental activities were identified and a buddy system was established, coupling high performers and low performers. In one case, a particularly low-performing salesperson with a major account became the focus of "shape up or ship out." The coaching here also entailed developing approaches to get cooperation from the engineering staff to enhance sales effectiveness. Periodic meetings were scheduled with the engineering staff explaining technical issues to the sales staff and at the same time the sales staff describing client needs. These meetings enhanced the understanding between sales and engineering and led to better cooperation and better sales. As the sales results began to improve, the sales manager began to trust managing by objectives rather than micromanaging behavior.

**Getting an Executive on Board**

At the time that this executive was appointed as chief technology officer (CTO) and started a new position, a coach was engaged to facilitate the on-boarding process. The executive was new to the industry and had no prior relations with either the senior management of the company or members of his staff. As is typical of anyone who starts a new position, this executive was overwhelmed with a steep learning curve regarding people, projects and organization structure. The primary role of the coach in this engagement was to help clarify priorities of relationship building, organizational clarification and work product deliverables. This coaching engagement provided weekly support to the executive to explore the many issues with which he had to deal.

The coach asked numerous questions of the executive in order to understand the environment at his new company. The executive was able to see his situation more clearly as a result of these questions and was able to formulate action steps in order to get himself functioning fully in his new position. An early request from the executive's boss for a revised budget and an update on projects provided a basis for the CTO to accelerate all of the on-boarding activities that are essential to success in a new position. The coach guided the executive to maintain focus on sorting out priorities, building important relationships, and energizing his team. The result of this coaching engagement was an efficient and effective start-up for this executive in his new position. Approximately one year after he started with this company, his responsibilities were expanded.

### Getting the Successor Ready

A financial institution with a fully developed succession planning process had identified a very strong and competent executive as the chosen successor to the current chief information officer (CIO). But there was one behavior pattern of this deputy CIO that was annoying to numerous people. At meetings at which important issues were being discussed and decisions were being made, the deputy CIO would listen for about twenty minutes and would then announce his idea as to the appropriate solution to the issue being discussed. This preempting of the full presentation and ensuing discussion raised many people's hackles at these meetings. After the presentation was completed and all participants had discussed the issue, the solution that was adopted almost always coincided with the early recommendation from the deputy CIO. In spite of being a thought leader, people were still annoyed at his behavior.

Once this issue was out in the open and discussed by the CIO, HR, the coach and the executive together, it was a matter of singular focus on this one issue. The first step was to adopt the coaching goal to allow presentations to be completed and then use persuasion as opposed to abruptly co-opting a discussion.

The next phase was to find an action plan to satisfy this goal. The executive was able to articulate his sense of wasting time by listening to the whole presentation when he already knew the answer. The coach pointed out that the presentation and the meeting ran its full course even after he made his early recommendations. Therefore, in fact, the executive was not saving any time for himself or others. After examining different approaches, it was agreed that the executive would try asking questions of the group such that the answers to the questions would lead the group toward the solution that the executive had in mind. The executive was very nimble and quickly developed approaches to raising questions that helped solve the problem.

This executive experienced two positive outcomes as he learned a new way to convey information to a group. First, the irritation the group had experienced in the past was no longer an issue. Secondly, as an unexpected by-product, the meetings became shorter. Approximately six months after the coaching engagement, the deputy CIO was promoted to CIO.

### Enhancing Influence and Delegation

At a large financial services institution, a vice president had responsibility for protecting the integrity of systems, data and operations. Two of the coaching goals for this executive included (1) avoiding confrontation when trying to influence others and (2) elevating his comfort with his managerial status to allow for more delegation so as to allow for, in turn, more time for strategic issues.

To reduce the need for confrontation when trying to influence people, the executive was encouraged to use questions as a tool to identify flaws in other's suggestions. This communication style led to more information being available and others being able to see the problems associated with their line of reasoning. The need for confrontation was notably reduced.

To elevate his comfort with his managerial status and to satisfy his responsibility for strategic leadership, the executive was encouraged to regularly and carefully examine his calendar to identify the high-value activities for which his involvement was important and correspondingly delegate those activities that could be handled by subordinates and were not central to a focus on strategic management of information security. The coach and executive together developed a set of guidelines for future behavior and the result was less confrontation and more time for strategy.

### Improving Profitability by Changing Management Style

Before the coaching engagement began, this head of trading was described as, "probably too nice, not tough enough and not quick enough in making decisions."

During the initial process of getting to know the executive, the issue of department profitability came to the surface. During the prior two years, the department had flat revenues and was barely profitable. Rather than examining the behavioral characteristics just described, the focus of the coaching was on the urgency of profitability.

In reviewing his business activities to find ways to increase revenue and profits, the coach and the executive agreed to action steps for the executive. To implement the action steps, there were situations in which he needed to be tough and in which he needed to make decisions promptly. The result of the focus on profit brought significant changes in his management style. By midyear, revenues had doubled and profit had increased sixfold, albeit over a very modest base. The coach helped the executive be fully aware of changes in management style and its associated impact on business performance. This pattern of improved financial results continued for the balance of the year.

# Appendix C
# Finding and
# Selecting a Coach

The safest way to find a great coach is through referrals. If this is your first effort to consider an executive coach, seek out recommendations from the Human Resources departments of nearby companies whose performance you respect.

A second source to turn to is the International Coaching Federation (ICF) (www.coachfederation.org). ICF provides a database of coaches that is searchable by areas of interest, coach's background, coaching method, gender, language and location. The seventeen areas of interest listed range from leadership and management skills to family issues and health and fitness. Choices for a coach's background include CEO, consultant, inventor, sales manager, and dozens more. The six coaching methods include in-person, telephone, and e-mail.

A Google search on the term "executive coaching" returns over seven million matching sites, an overwhelming amount of information. If you narrow the search to "executive coach [city]" and insert the name of your city, the number of sites is much more manageable. For example, "New York City" returns four hundred sites and "St. Louis" returns twenty five.

This field is only about twenty five years old and lacks any universal licensing or certification. There are numerous certification programs of varying depth and quality. Certification and training or education are no substitute for business experience, maturity, interpersonal skills and coaching experience, but it does offer a modicum of comfort as to the readiness of an individual to serve as a coach.

Once you have identified a potential executive coach, here are some questions that you might ask to determine whether the coach is a good fit for your organization's needs:

- How long have you been coaching?
- Approximately how many people have you coached?
- Describe a profile of people you have been coaching.
- What training or certification do you have in coaching?
- Describe your typical executive coaching program.

Once you have a chance to meet with a potential executive coach, it is very reasonable to ask for some references, although some executive coaches will be reluctant to give references as a matter of confidentiality.

Amazon.com reveals over two hundred books on the subject. The books cover methodology, guidelines for building a coaching business, many different flavors of coaching (e.g. lifestyle, career, and management), and examples of outstanding coaching cases. Some are noted in the bibliography.

# Bibliography

Crane, Thomas C., with Lerissa Patrick. *The Heart of Coaching: Using Transformational Coaching to Create a High-Performance Culture.* Rev. ed. San Diego: FTA Press, 2002.

Downey, Myles. *Effective Coaching: Lessons from the Coach's Coach.* 2nd ed. New York: Texere, 2003.

Goldsmith, Marshall, Laurence Lyons, and Alyssa Freas, eds. *Coaching for Leadership: How the World's Greatest Coaches Help Leaders Learn.* San Francisco: Jossey-Bass/Pfeiffer, 2000.

Hammond, Sue Annis, and Cathy Royal, eds. *Lessons from the Field: Applying Appreciative Inquiry,* Plano, Tex.: Thin Book, 1998.

Hargrove, Robert. *Masterful Coaching.* New York: Wiley, 2003.

Shula, Don, and Ken Blanchard, *Everyone's a Coach.* New York: HarperBusiness, 1995.

Skiffington, Suzanne, and Perry Zeus. *Behavioral Coaching.* New York: McGraw-Hill, 2003.

Ting, Sharon, and Peter Scisco, eds. *The CCL Handbook of Coaching: A Guide for Leader Coaching.* San Francisco: Jossey-Bass, 2006.

Whitworth, Laura, Karen Kimsey-House, Henry Kimsey-House, and Phillip Sandahl. *Co-Active Coaching: New Skills for Coaching People Toward Success in Work and Life.* Mountain View, Calif.: Davies-Black, 1998.

Witherspoon, Robert, and Randall P. White. *Four Essential Ways That Coaching Can Help Executives.* Greensboro, N.C.: Center for Creative Leadership, 1998.

Zeus, Perry, and Suzanne Skiffington. *The Complete Guide to Coaching at Work.* New York: McGraw-Hill, 2003.

# Fedcap

## Half of the profits from the sale of this book go to Fedcap.

Fedcap is a nonprofit organization located in New York City for over 70 years and that has been a leader in developing training and employment programs for people with disabilities and other significant barriers to employment. Their mission is to help people with barriers to employment find and keep meaningful jobs so that they can achieve independence, support themselves and their families, and actively participate in their communities. Fedcap does this by providing vocational evaluations to determine clients' interests and aptitudes, and job training in preparation for specific careers including custodian, office support, culinary arts, security guard, and home health aide. Fedcap also offers ongoing job support to help transition individuals into the world of work, whether a client chooses to work in one of Fedcap's employment programs or at a job in the community. One division of Fedcap assembles special safety devices for the U.S. government that are used by military personnel that would help locate them if they are shot down or lost at sea. Fedcap provides custodial services and back office mailroom management for many federal and state buildings in the New York City area including court houses, the Statue of Liberty and Ellis Island, the New York City Fire Department, and the Long Island Railroad at Penn Station. There is also a day program for people with a history of mental illness that helps members remain stable, focused, functioning members of the community, and when participants are ready, prepares them for employment again. The organization does very meaningful work and has been chosen as a national Center of Excellence for its largest business service activity, namely the custodial business. The organization has an annual budget in excess of $60 million.

The author has served on Fedcap's Board of Directors for eight years and has served as President of the Board since 2003. For more information, please look at www.fedcap.org.

# Your Feedback

Brenner Executive Resources, Inc.
1230 Avenue of the Americas 7$^{th}$ Floor
New York, NY 10020
Phone: 917-639-4035
E-mail: michael@brennerresources.com
Web site: www.brennerresources.com

The firm offers executive coaching to corporations based on the ideas in this book with a total focus on improving managerial excellence.

I hope this book has been helpful to you. I would welcome any feedback and examples of coaching for managerial excellence. If there is any material that you wish had been included, please let me know.

Inquiries are welcome and all inquiries will be answered.

# About the Author

Active in human resource consulting for over thirty years, Michael Brenner now specializes in coaching individuals and groups. He is a Certified Master Coach and coaches to support the general development of senior executives, to enhance the performance of highly valued executives who are below their full potential and to build high-performing teams. He has served clients in media and entertainment, financial services, technology and manufacturing. In addition to his coaching, he participated earlier in consulting about performance evaluation, compensation, and staffing and has had extensive experience in handling senior-level executive searches. Besides formal coaching training, his background includes three years as associate professor of management at the graduate business school at NYU, adjunct management teaching at the graduate business school at Fordham University, and work as a management development trainer at Ernst & Young.

Mr. Brenner founded Brenner Executive Resources, Inc. in January 1999 to pursue coaching and executive search independently. Since 2003, he has focused exclusively on coaching and has worked with hundreds of people. Early in 2004, Mr. Brenner was appointed regional managing director for executive coaching for the New York area of Korn/Ferry International and now continues to serve as a senior executive coach for Korn/Ferry clients in addition to continuing to operate his own firm.

His twenty years of executive search experience includes eight years ending in 1999 at Hudson Highland Group (formerly known as Lamalie Associates, then the fifth-largest search firm in the United States) where he was a senior partner, a director, and the practice leader. Mr. Brenner earlier was also a partner at Canny Bowen, a boutique executive search firm, for five years. In addition, his career also includes seven years, five in management, in information systems at Bell Telephone Laboratories and five years in human resources at Ernst & Young.

Mr. Brenner earned a Bachelor of Science in Industrial Management at the Sloan School at MIT and a Doctor of Engineering in Industrial Engineering with a minor in psychology from Johns Hopkins University. He served in the U.S. Army Signal Corps as a second lieutenant. Mr. Brenner has attended coach training with the Behavioral Coaching Institute, Coach Training Institute and is a member of the International Coach Federation. He has been invited as a speaker on executive coaching at professional conferences and universities. He is a charter member of the Human Resource Executive Forum, was a member of the Society for Human Resource Management

(SHRM) and served as president of its New York Chapter and is active in the Society for Information Management (SIM). He has founded the New York Executive Coaching Network as a professional forum for New York based executive coaches. Mr. Brenner is also president of the Board of Directors of Fedcap, a not-for-profit organization with an annual budget over $60 million that trains and employs individuals with disabilities.

Lightning Source UK Ltd.
Milton Keynes UK
UKOW050223280613

212886UK00001B/24/A